BECAUSE OF YOU

CELEBRATING THE DIFFERENCE YOU MAKE

Compiled by Dan Zadra with Katie Lambert
Designed by Kobi Yamada and Steve Potter

COMPENDIUM™
PUBLISHING

live inspired.

For Mom and Dad. Because of You. With love, Kobi

ACKNOWLEDGEMENTS

These quotations were gathered lovingly but unscientifically over several years and/or contributed by many friends or acquaintances. Some arrived—and survived in our files—on scraps of paper and may therefore be imperfectly worded or attributed. To the authors, contributors and original sources, our thanks, and where appropriate, our apologies. —The editors

WITH SPECIAL THANKS TO

Jason Aldrich, Gerry Baird, Jay Baird, Neil Beaton, Doug Cruickshank, Jim Darragh, Jennifer & Matt Ellison, Josie & Rob Estes, Michael Flynn, Jennifer Hurwitz, Liam Lavery, Connie McMartin, Cristal & Brad Olberg, Janet Potter & Family, Aimee Rawlins, Diane Roger, Drew Wilkie, Jenica Wilkie, Robert & Mary Anne Wilkie, Heidi & Shale Yamada, Justi, Tote & Caden Yamada, Robert & Val Yamada, Kaz, Kristin, Kyle & Kendyl Yamada, Tai & Joy Yamada, Anne Zadra, August & Arline Zadra and Dan Zadra.

CREDITS

Compiled by Dan Zadra

Designed by Kobi Yamada and Steve Potter

ISBN: 1-932319-19-0

Printed in China

CELEBRATING
THE DIFFERENCE
YOU MAKE

BECAUSE OF YOU

It's our dream that this book will somehow find its way into the hands and hearts of the right people—the people who are the everyday heroes in our lives.

Because we live or work side-by-side with them, it's easy to find our heroes—we all know them when we see them—but it's not so easy to thank them. How do you properly thank people who often do so much, with so little, for so long?

The quotations in this book are not about fame or acclaim, they are about caring and accomplishment. They are not about well-known people making a fortune, they are about everyday people making a difference. You know who they are, we all do. In every corner of every neighborhood, community or company, there are people who quietly and persistently brighten the lives of those around them, but who are seldom celebrated or applauded.

What kind of people will make your everyday heroes list? The people on my list will probably never see their names printed in *Who's Who*, but they'll definitely find kindred spirits among the people quoted in *Because Of You*. Among them are a teacher who inspired, a mentor who cared, a friend who understood, a partner who persevered, a client who believed, an investor who trusted, a vendor who helped, a minister who guided, a physician who triumphed, a nurse who comforted, a family who loved and sacrificed, and a staff of loyal and talented people who endured and prevailed.

THANK YOU FOR MAKING THE DIFFERENCE.
IT ALL HAPPENS BECAUSE OF YOU.

Dan Zadra

BECAUSE OF YOU

WE CAN
DO MORE THAN
DREAM, WE CAN
IMAGINE.

Hope is a waking dream.

–ARISTOTLE

Life is to be lived; there is no help for it.

–ELEANOR ROOSEVELT

Careful what you set your heart upon.
For it surely shall be yours.

–RALPH WALDO EMERSON

CELEBRATING THE DIFFERENCE YOU MAKE

It matters not
how long we live but how.

—PHILIP JAMES BAILEY

We can't do much about
the length of our lives, but we can do
plenty about its width and depth.

—EVAN ESAR

Our aspirations are our possibilities.

—ROBERT BROWNING

The purpose of life is
a life of purpose.

—ROBERT BYRNE

We must create our own world.

—LOUISE NEVELSON

Our main task is
to give birth to ourselves.

—ERICH FROMM

CELEBRATING THE DIFFERENCE YOU MAKE

I have always preferred
having wings to having things.

—PAT SCHROEDER

When I asked for all things, so that
I might enjoy life…I was given life, so
that I might enjoy all things.

—UNKNOWN

If you have a dream, you have everything.
If you have everything and no dream,
then everything means nothing.

—EDGE KEYNOTE

Most people don't know that
there are angels whose only job is to
make sure you don't get too comfortable
and fall asleep and miss your life.

—BRIAN ANDREAS, "STILL MOSTLY TRUE"

I began to realize that life is
a growth stage I'm going through.

—ELLEN GOODMAN

I now see my life, not as the slow shaping
of achievement to fit my preconceived
purposes, but as the gradual discovery
of a purpose which I did not know.

—JOANNA FIELD

CELEBRATING THE DIFFERENCE YOU MAKE

If you are going to do anything with life,
you sometimes have to move away from it,
beyond the usual measurements. You must
occasionally follow visions and dreams.

—BEDE JARRETT

12

A vision foretells what may be ours.
With a great mental picture in mind we
begin to go from one accomplishment to
another, using the materials about us
only as stepping stones to that which is
higher, better and more satisfying.

—KATHERINE LOGAN

It is difficult to say what is impossible
for us. The dream of yesterday is the hope
of today and the reality of tomorrow.

—ROBERT GODDARD

Never cut loose from your longings.

—AMOS OZ

No one should negotiate
their dreams. Dreams must be free
to flee and fly high. You should never
agree to surrender your aspirations.

—JESSE JACKSON

If you do not hope, you will
not find what is beyond your hopes.

—ST. CLEMENT

Always keep one still,
secret spot where dreams may go and,
sheltered so, may thrive and grow.

—LOUISE PRISCOLL

Cherish your visions, your ideals,
the music that stirs in your heart.
If you remain true to them, your world will
at last be built.

—JAMES ALLEN

CELEBRATING THE DIFFERENCE YOU MAKE

WE CAN
DO MORE
THAN PROMISE,
WE CAN COMMIT.

Right now is a good time.

—TOTE YAMADA

I have always had a dread
of becoming a passenger in life.

—MARGRETHE OF DENMARK

It's time to start living the life
we've imagined.

—HENRY JAMES

Do what you can, with what
you have, where you are.

—THEODORE ROOSEVELT

Truth and life are all around you.
What matters is where and when
you decide to put your focus.

—ROGER VON OECH

A hundred times every day I remind myself
that life depends on the labors of others,
living and dead, and that I must exert
myself in order to give in the measure as
I have received and am still receiving.

—ALBERT EINSTEIN

It is easy to be
brave from a safe distance.

—AESOP

A ship in port is safe, but that's
not what ships are made for.

—ADMIRAL GRACE HOPPER

You can clutch the past so tightly
to your chest that it leaves your arms
too full to embrace the present.

—JAN GLIDEWELL

There will always be a frontier where there is an open mind and a willing hand.

—CHARLES F. KETTERING

There has been a calculated risk in every stage of American development—pioneers who were not afraid of the wilderness, business people who were not afraid of failure, dreamers who were not afraid of action.

—GIL ATKINSON

To begin is the most important part of any quest, and by far the most courageous.

—PLATO

CELEBRATING THE DIFFERENCE YOU MAKE

Reality always
forms around commitment.

—KOBI YAMADA

Be assured that any worthwhile action
will create change and attract support.

—PHILIP MARVIN

Give thanks for unknown
blessings already on their way.

—NATIVE AMERICAN SAYING

BECAUSE OF YOU

WE CAN
DO MORE
THAN BELIEVE,
WE CAN CREATE.

The ancestor of every
beautiful action is a creative thought.

—FRANK VIZARRE

Every candle ever lit; every home,
bridge, cathedral or city ever built;
every act of human kindness, discovery,
daring, artistry or advancement started
first in someone's imagination,
and then worked its way out.

—GIL ATKINSON

Imagination:
The art of seeing things invisible.

—JONATHAN SWIFT

22

The future cannot be predicted,
but futures can be invented. It is our
ability to invent the future which gives
us hope and makes us what we are.

—DENNIS GABOR

Live your life on purpose.

—DAN ZADRA

Hope is a good thing,
maybe the best of things,
and no good thing ever dies.

—SHAWSHANK REDEMPTION

Remember that yesterday's
answer may have nothing to do
with today's problem.

—DON WARD

Every great advance has issued
from a new audacity of imagination.

—JOHN DEWEY

An age is called Dark,
not because the light fails to shine,
but because people refuse to see it.

—JAMES A. MICHENER

I can believe anything
provided it is incredible.

—OSCAR WILDE

Two days before the Wright Brothers
made their historic takeoff at Kittyhawk
a Boston newspaper ran an article
proving that heavier-than-air flight
was "impossible."

—GREAT IDEAS

25

Always listen to the experts.
They'll tell you what can't be done
and why. Then go ahead and do it.

—DON WARD

Don't expect anything
original from an echo.

—JOANNA WICK

Do just once what others say
you can't do, and you will never pay
attention to their limitations again.

—EDMUND BROWN, JR.

See things as
you would have them be,
instead of as they are.

—ROBERT COLLIER

A hunch is creativity trying
to tell you something. It's the voice
of invention calling you forward.

—FRANK CAPRA

In my dream, the angel shrugged
and said, "If we fail this time,
it will be a failure of imagination."
And then she placed the world
gently in the palm of my hand.

—BRIAN ANDREAS, "STILL MOSTLY TRUE"

BECAUSE OF YOU

WE CAN
DO MORE THAN
BELONG, WE CAN
PARTICIPATE.

Nobody, but nobody,
can make it out here alone.

—MAYA ANGELOU

No matter what great things you may
accomplish in life, somebody helps you.

—WILMA RUDOLPH

You can dream, create, design,
and build the most wonderful idea in
the world, but it requires people
to make the dream a reality.

—WALT DISNEY

CELEBRATING THE DIFFERENCE YOU MAKE

Very few burdens
are heavy if everyone lifts.

—SY WISE

Combine two or more people in the
pursuit of a common purpose and you
can achieve more with less. Together we
are able to accomplish what none of us
could achieve alone.

—DAN ZADRA

You will rise by lifting others.

—ROBERT GREEN INGERSOLL

30

The Great Northern Geese travel
thousands of miles in perfect formation,
and therein lies the secret. As each of the
great birds moves its wings, it creates
a steady uplift for the bird behind it.
Formation flying is 70 percent more
efficient than flying alone.

LESSON:

People who share a common
direction and sense of community can
get where they're going quicker and
easier because they're traveling on the
strength of one another.

—GREAT NORTHERN GEESE, LESSON 1

Vital to every
worthwhile operation is cooperation.

—FRANK TYGER

Either we're pulling together
or we're pulling apart. There's really
no in-between.

—KOBI YAMADA

32

This is a team. We're trying to go to
the moon. If you can't put someone up,
please don't put them down.

—NASA MOTTO

Those with whom we work
look to us for heat as well as light.

—WOODROW WILSON

The object is not to see through one
another, but to see one another through.

—PETER DEVRIES

People must believe in each
other, and feel that it can be done
and must be done; in that way they
are enormously strong. We must
keep up each other's courage.

—VINCENT VAN GOGH

When people go to work,
they shouldn't have to leave
their hearts at home.

—BETTY BENDER

Loyalty means not that I agree with
everything you say, or that I believe you
are always right. Loyalty means that I
share a common ideal with you and that,
regardless of minor differences, we
strive for it, shoulder to shoulder,
confident in one another's good faith,
trust, constancy and affection.

—DR. KARL MENNINGER

Progress results only from the fact
that there are some men and women
who refuse to believe that what they
know to be right cannot be done.

—RUSSELL DAVENPORT

As life is action and passion, it is
required of us that we should share the
action and passion of our time at peril
of being judged not to have lived.

—OLIVER WENDELL HOLMES

There is somebody smarter
than any of us, and that is all of us.

—MICHAEL NOLAN

No one can be the best at
everything. But when all of us combine
our talents, we can and will be the best at
virtually anything.

—DAN ZADRA

36

Life is like the car pool lane.
The only way to get to your destination
quickly is to take some people with you.

—PETER WARD

The best hope of solving
all our problems lies in harnessing
the diversity, the energy and the
creativity of all our people.

—ROGER WILKINS

Never doubt that a small group
of thoughtful, committed people can
change the world. Indeed, it is the
only thing that ever has.

—MARGARET MEAD

BECAUSE OF YOU

WE CAN
DO MORE THAN
WORK, WE CAN
GROW.

We work to
become, not just to acquire.

—ELBERT HUBBARD

People are saying,
"I want a company and a job
that values me as much as I value it.
I want something in my life not just to
invest my time in, but to believe in."

—ANITA RODDICK

To make a living is no longer enough.
Work also has to make a life.

—PETER DRUCKER

CELEBRATING THE DIFFERENCE YOU MAKE

The real secret of joy in work is
contained in one word—excellence. To know
how to do something well is to enjoy it.

—PEARL BUCK

Start a crusade in your life—
to dare to be your best.

—WILLIAM DANFORTH

Failures are few among people who
have found a work they enjoy enough to
do it well. You invest time in your work;
invest love in it too.

—CLARENCE FLYNN

We cannot become what we
need to be by remaining what we are.

—MAX DE PREE

I will study and get ready and
someday my chance will come.

—ABRAHAM LINCOLN

If I miss three days of practice,
my audience knows it. If I miss two
days, my critics know it. If I miss
one day, I know it.

—IGNACE PADEREWSKI, CONCERT PIANIST

When you respond to something
because it's so beautiful, you're really
looking at the soul of the person
who made it.

—ALICE WALKER

We can paint a great picture
on a small canvas.

—C.D. WARNER

You can excel with very little experience,
provided you have a very large heart.

—KOBI YAMADA

Act as if what you do
makes a difference. It does.

—WILLIAM JAMES

The world is moved along, not
only by the mighty shoves of its heroes,
but also by the aggregate of the tiny
pushes of each honest worker.

—HELEN KELLER

There is no such thing as
an insignificant improvement.

—TOM PETERS

Our nation advances only by the
extra achievements of the individual.
You are the individual.

—CHARLES TOWNE

Nothing works unless you do.

—NIDO QUBEIN

44

As you cherish the things
most worthwhile in your family life,
cherish the things most worthwhile
in your work life.

—WILLIAM GIVEN

Everyone is trying to accomplish
something big, not realizing that life
is made up of little things.

—FRANK A. CLARK

The world knows nothing
of its greatest people.

—HENRY TAYLOR

Each day unknown men and women
do great deeds, speak great words and
suffer noble sorrows.

—CHARLES READE

Quality is not just a chart,
or a standard, or a specification—
it's a state of mind, a commitment,
a responsibility, a spirit. It's a way
of doing, being and living.

—DON GALER

46

Do something brilliant every day.
Make a great meal tonight. Sell something
in a dynamic way. Spectacularly deliver a
presentation. Tell an outstanding joke.
Slash through a difficult obstacle.
Dream a wonderful dream.

—ROGER VON OECH

Encourage each other to become
the best you can be. Celebrate what
you want to see more of.

—TOM PETERS

When we put a limit on what we will do,
we put a limit on what we can do.

—CHARLES SCHWAB

If everyone is moving forward together,
then success will take care of itself.

—HENRY FORD

CELEBRATING THE DIFFERENCE YOU MAKE

When one of the Great Northern Geese
falls out of formation, it suddenly feels
the drag and resistance of trying to fly
alone and quickly rejoins the formation
to take advantage of the lifting power
of the bird immediately in front.

LESSON:

If we apply the strategy of the geese,
we will stay in formation with those
who are ahead of where we want
to go and be willing to accept their
help as well as give it to others.

—GREAT NORTHERN GEESE, LESSON II

One person can make a difference,
and every person must try.

—JOHN F. KENNEDY

When you do the best you can,
you never know what miracle is wrought
in your life, or in the life of another.

—HELEN KELLER

Leave your story
better than you found it.

—M.H. WARD

BECAUSE OF YOU

WE CAN
DO MORE THAN
LEARN, WE CAN
TEACH.

There's always one moment in life when
the door opens and lets the future in.

—GRAHAM GREEN

The dream begins
with a person who believes in you,
who tugs and pushes and leads you to
the next plateau, sometimes poking you
with a sharp stick called "truth."

—DAN RATHER

Hopefully, your education
left much to be desired.

—ALAN GREGG

We are all teachers, or should be.
Anyone who relays experience to another
person is a teacher. Not to transmit your
experience is to betray it.

—ELIE WIESEL

Mentor each other unselfishly.

—HEROIC ENVIRONMENTS

Dedicate some of your life to teaching
others. Your dedication will not be a
sacrifice. It will be an exhilarating
experience because it is intense effort
applied toward a meaningful end.

—DR. THOMAS DOOLEY

The best minute you spend
is the one you invest in people.

—KEN BLANCHARD

Teaching is not the filling
of the pail but the lighting of the fire.

—WILLIAM BUTLER YEATS

53

In the end, you can
only teach the things that you are.

—MAX LEARNER

We must have places where
children can have a whole group
of adults they can trust.

—MARGARET MEAD

I think teachers and leaders
should encourage the next generation not
just to follow, but to overtake.

—ANITA RODDICK

54

There are only two lasting bequests
we can hope to give our children:
One of these is roots, the other is wings.

—HODDING CARTER

Some parents bring their children up,
and some let them down.

—CARRIE SULLIVAN

Presence is more than just being there.

—MALCOLM FORBES

You may have tangible
wealth untold. You may have caskets
of jewels and coffers of gold. But richer
than I you can never be; I had
a mother who read to me.

—STRICKLAND GILLILAN

We are drowning in
information but starving for knowledge.

—RUTHERFORD ROGERS

The future is in the hands
of those who can give tomorrow's
generations valid reasons to
live and hope.

—TEILHARD DE CHARDIN

He taught me to run high on my toes.
I will always remember his words:
"Run proud and remember you are alive."

—BRIAN ANDREAS, "STILL MOSTLY TRUE"

CELEBRATING THE DIFFERENCE YOU MAKE

BECAUSE OF YOU

WE CAN DO
MORE THAN LEAD,
WE CAN INSPIRE.

We have to get people
excited again about using their talents.

—PAT CARRIGAN

We all need to believe
in what we're doing.

—ALLAN GILMOUR

58

You cannot kindle a fire in any other heart
until it is burning in your own.

—BEN SWEETLAND

Everyone leads.
Leadership is action, not position.

—DONALD H. MCGANNON

The great leader is not
the one in the spotlight, he is the
one leading the applause.

—COMMITMENT TO EXCELLENCE

If he works for you,
then you work for him.

—JAPANESE PROVERB

"We" rather than "I."

—CHARLES GARFIELD

The best leaders are not interested
in selling their own ideas, but in finding
the best ideas. They are not interested in
having their own way, but in
finding the best way.

—COMMITMENT TO TEAMWORK

The first and last task of a leader
is to keep hope alive—the hope that
we can and will find our way
through to a better world.

—JOHN W. GARDNER

Never give up on anybody.

—HUBERT H. HUMPHREY

Everyone is a winner.
Some people are disguised as losers.
Don't let their appearances fool you.

—KEN BLANCHARD

There is nothing so rewarding as
to make people realize that they are
worthwhile in this world.

—BOB ANDERSON

The greatest good we can do
for others is not to share our riches
but to reveal theirs.

—GIL ATKINSON

When you look for the good in others, you
discover the best in yourself.

—MARTIN WALSH

Treat people as they are, and they
remain that way. Treat them as though
they are already what they can be,
and you help them become what
they are capable of becoming.

—GOETHE

Encourage one another. Many times a
word of praise or thanks or appreciation
or cheer has kept people on their feet.

—CHARLES SWINDOLL

You can work miracles
by expressing faith in others. To get
the best out of people, choose to think and
believe the best about them.

—BOB MOAWAD

There is more hunger for love and
appreciation in this world than for bread.

—MOTHER TERESA

Each flock of Great Northern Geese
is its own unique community.
Each flock finds its own rhythm.
The pulsating sound of the great wings
beating together excites and energizes
the entire formation, replenishing their
courage and stamina. The geese
honk from behind to encourage those
up front to keep up their speed.

LESSON:
We need to make sure our
honking from behind is energizing and
encouraging, and not something else.

—GREAT NORTHERN GEESE, LESSON III

A company's character is
known by the people it keeps.

—JOHN RUSKIN

Heart, instinct, principles.

—BLAISE PASCAL

A mighty flame follows
a tiny spark.

—DANTE

You can't stop people from thinking—
but you can start them.

—FRANK DUSCH

Just remember: People tend to resist that
which is forced upon them. People tend to
support that which they help to create.

—VINCE PFAFF

66

One person may supply the idea for
a company, community or nation, but
what gives the idea its force is
a community of dreams.

—ANDRE MALRAUX

CELEBRATING THE DIFFERENCE YOU MAKE

Trust is the conviction that the leader means what he or she says. It is a belief in two old-fashioned qualities called consistency and integrity. Trust opens the door to change.

—PETER DRUCKER

If people are coming to work excited...if they're making mistakes freely and fearlessly...if they're having fun...if they're concentrating on doing things, rather than preparing reports and going to meetings—then somewhere you have leaders.

—ROBERT TOWNSEND

BECAUSE OF YOU

WE CAN DO
MORE THAN
TOLERATE,
WE CAN
REACH OUT.

If only all the hands
that reach could touch.

—MARY A. LOBERG

Only connect.

—E.M. FORSTER

What a wonderful miracle,
if only we could look through
each other's eyes for an instant.

—HENRY DAVID THOREAU

CELEBRATING THE DIFFERENCE YOU MAKE

It is never too late
to give up our prejudices.

—HENRY DAVID THOREAU

If we have no peace,
it is because we have forgotten
that we belong to each other.

—MOTHER TERESA

Injustice anywhere is
a threat to justice everywhere.

—MARTIN LUTHER KING, JR.

Fear makes strangers
out of people who should be friends.

—SHIRLEY MACLAINE

We are, of course, a nation of differences.
Those differences don't make us weak.
They're the source of our strength.

—JIMMY CARTER

With so many spectacular colors
in the world, it's a shame to make
everything black and white.

—DENNIS R. LITTLE

Each person represents a world
in us, a world possibly not born
until they arrive, and it is only by this
meeting that a new world is born.

—ANAIS NIN

. He drew a circle that shut me out—
heretic, rebel, a thing to flout. But love
and I had the will to win; we drew
a circle that took him in.

—EDWIN MARKHAM

What a world this
would be if we just built bridges
instead of walls.

—CARLOS RAMIREZ

We must be the change
we wish to see in the world.

—GANDHI

The time is always right
to do what is right.

—MARTIN LUTHER KING, JR.

We don't learn to know people through their coming to us. To find out what sort of people they are, we must go to them.

—GOETHE

Empathy is patiently and sincerely seeing the world through the other person's eyes. It is not learned in school; it is cultivated over a lifetime.

—ALBERT EINSTEIN

Laughter is the best communion of all.

—ROBERT FULGHUM

There is no such thing as
"them and us." In a world this
size there can only be "we"–
all of us working together.

—DON WARD

If there must be a stereotype,
let it have nothing to do with race,
creed, color, sex or advantage. Let it
have everything to do with effort, energy,
ideas, commitment and capabilities.

—DAN ZADRA

As a kid I learned that
my brother and I could walk forever
on a railroad track and never fall off—
if we just reached across the track
and held each other's hand.

—STEVE POTTER

If you don't know the kind of person
I am, and if I don't know the kind of
person you are, a pattern that others
made may prevail in the world—
and we may miss our star.

—WILLIAM STAFFORD

CELEBRATING THE DIFFERENCE YOU MAKE

BECAUSE OF YOU

WE CAN
DO MORE
THAN CARE,
WE CAN HELP.

There must be more
to life than having everything.

—MAURICE SENDAK

We are all here on earth to
help others; what on earth the others
are here for I don't know.

—W.H. AUDEN

Every day is an opportunity
to change things for the better.

—MICHAEL PIVEC

Things you do for other people are
usually among the best things you do.

—TO YOUR SUCCESS

The greatest tragedy is indifference.

—THE RED CROSS

Give what you have. To someone, it may
be better than you dare think.

—LONGFELLOW

I expect to pass through this world
but once. Any good therefore that I can
do, or any kindness that I can show, let me
do it now. Let me not defer or neglect it,
for I shall not pass this way again.

—UNKNOWN

The only justification we have
to look down on someone is because
we are about to pick him up.

—JESSE JACKSON

The measure of life is not
its duration but its donation.

—PETER MARSHALL

Great opportunities
to help others seldom come, but
small ones surround us every day.

—SALLY KOCH

When it comes to doing good
things for others, some people
will stop at nothing.

—PALOMINO

Nice how we never get dizzy
from doing good turns.

—GEORGE BENGIS

CELEBRATING THE DIFFERENCE YOU MAKE

When one of the Great Northern
Geese gets sick, wounded or shot down,
two geese drop out of formation and
follow it down to help and protect it.
They stay with it until it is able to fly again
or dies. They then launch out on their
own to join another formation, or they
catch up with their own flock.

LESSON:

If we have as much empathy and
loyalty as geese, we too will stand
by each other in difficult times,
as well as when we are strong.

—GREAT NORTHERN GEESE, LESSON IV

The only gift is a portion of thyself.

—EMERSON

What I spent, I had.
What I kept, I lost.
What I gave, I have.

—HENRY BUCHER

We make a living by what we get.
But we make a life by what we give.

—UNKNOWN

The best portion of a good person's life,
those little nameless acts of kindness.

—UNKNOWN

Unselfish acts are the real miracles out of
which all the reported miracles grow.

—EMERSON

We must not only give what we have;
we must also give what we are.

—CARDINAL MERCIER

CELEBRATING THE DIFFERENCE YOU MAKE

BECAUSE OF YOU

WE CAN
DO MORE THAN
CRITICIZE,
WE CAN SERVE.

We have it in our power
to begin the world again.

—THOMAS PAINE, 1778

Life is made up of
constant calls to action.

—LEARNED HAND

How wonderful it is that nobody
need wait a single moment before
starting to improve the world.

—ANNE FRANK

Changing one small thing
for the better is worth more than
proving a thousand people wrong.

—ANTHONY PIVEC

We must care about the world
of our children and grandchildren,
a world we may never see.

—BERTRAND RUSSELL

Plant trees, under whose
shade you do not expect to sit.

—NELSON HENDERSON

I am tired of hearing that our
country doesn't work—it isn't supposed
to work. We are supposed to work it.

—ALEXANDER WOOLCOTT

If we want to make something
really superb of our community
and this planet, there is nothing
whatsoever that can stop us.

—SHEPHERD MEAD

If everyone sweeps in front of their door,
the whole city will be clean.

—URBAN PROVERB

88

Each of us is connected to all living
things whether we are aware of this
beautiful fact or not. And should you
ever begin to feel that you are becoming
separated from the world, you are simply
self-deceived, for you could no more do
this than a wave could separate itself from
the ocean and still be a wave.

—GERALD JAMPOLSKY

Seven national crimes:
I don't think. I don't know. I don't care.
I am too busy. I leave well enough alone.
I have no time to read and find out.
I am not interested.

—WILLIAM BOETCKER

The real friend of his country
is the person who believes in
excellence, seeks for it, fights for it,
defends it and tries to produce it.

—MORLEY CALLAGHAN

90

The difference between
what we do and what we are
capable of doing would solve most
of the world's problems.

—GANDHI

Our world is saved
one or two people at a time.

—ANDRE GIDE

If you think you are too small
to be effective, you have never been
in bed with a mosquito.

—BETTY REESE

Pray for the dead
and fight like hell for the living.

—LINDA ATKINSON

It isn't difficult to make a buck,
but it's tough to make a difference.

—TOM BROKAW

I am only one, but still I am one.
I cannot do everything, but still I can
do something. And because I cannot do
everything, I will not refuse to do
the something that I can do.

—HELEN KELLER

From now on, any definition of a
successful life must include serving others.

—GEORGE BUSH

WE CAN
DO MORE THAN
LOVE, WE CAN
BE LOVED.

We relish news of our
heroes, forgetting that we are
extraordinary to somebody too.

—HELEN HAYES

He liked to like people,
therefore people liked him.

—MARK TWAIN

There are no strangers—
only friends we have not met.

—FRANK VIZARRE

A friend is one who knows all
about you and loves you just the same.

—ELBERT HUBBARD

It takes a long time
to grow an old friend.

—JOHN LEONARD

Count your nights by stars, not shadows.
Count your days by smiles, not tears.
And on any birthday morning,
count your age by friends, not years.

—UNKNOWN

When one will not,
two cannot quarrel.

—SPANISH PROVERB

Always forgive your enemies;
nothing annoys them so much.

—OSCAR WILDE

It is by forgiving that one is forgiven.

—MOTHER TERESA

Love is not a competitive sport.

—LEO BUSCAGLIA

No matter how much cats fight,
there always seem to be plenty of kittens.

—ABRAHAM LINCOLN

Love is such a big word,
it really should have more letters.

—KOBI YAMADA

Love cures people–
both the ones who give it and
the ones who receive it.

—DR. CARL MENNINGER

When it comes to giving love,
the opportunities are endless
and we are all gifted.

—LEO BUSCAGLIA

Where you find no love, put love,
and you will find love.

—JOHN OF THE CROSS

The loving are the daring.

—BAYARD TAYLOR

It is not so difficult to develop a
loving attitude toward yourself and others.
Rather than searching for shortcomings,
love watches for any sign of light and
strength. It sees how far each one has
come, not how far he has to go.

—EDGE KEYNOTE

99

Today say "I love you" to those you love.
The eternal silence is long enough to be
silent in, and that awaits us all.

—GEORGE ELIOT

Where love reigns
the impossible may be attained.

—INDIAN PROVERB

The day will come when,
after harnessing space, the winds,
the tides and gravitation, we shall
harness for God the energies of love.
And on that day, for the second time
in the history of the world, we shall
have discovered fire.

—TIELHARD DE CHARDIN

BECAUSE OF YOU

WE CAN
DO MORE
THAN ENDURE,
WE CAN PREVAIL.

Adversity puts people
in touch with themselves.

—ROSE LANE

The hard times you go through
will lead to the good times you'll have.

—HENRY LITTLEFIELD

When you do not tire within but seek
the sweet satisfaction of your life and your
work, you are doing what you
were meant to be doing.

—GARY ZUKAV

Although the world is full of suffering,
it is also full of the overcoming of it.

—HELEN KELLER

One might take children's philosophy
to heart. They do not despise a bubble
because it burst; they immediately set
to work to blow another one.

—EDGE KEYNOTE

The sense of obligation to continue is
present in all of us. A duty to strive is the
duty of us all. I felt a call to that duty.

—ABRAHAM LINCOLN

CELEBRATING THE DIFFERENCE YOU MAKE

A thick skin is a gift from God.

—KONRAD ADENAUER

To wear your heart on your sleeve
isn't a very good plan. You should
wear it inside where it functions best.

—MARGARET THATCHER

Never attempt to bear
more than one kind of trouble at once.
Some people bear all three kinds:
all they have had, all they now have,
and all they expect to have.

—EDWARD EVERETT HALE

Nobody should move faster through
life than their guardian angel can fly.

—KOBI YAMADA

Life doesn't do anything to you,
it just reveals your spirit.

—UNKNOWN

Everyday courage has few witnesses.
But yours is no less noble because
no drum beats before you, and
no crowds shout your name.

—ROBERT LOUIS STEVENSON

CELEBRATING THE DIFFERENCE YOU MAKE

You always pass failure
on the way to success.

—MICKEY ROONEY

A person seldom makes
the same mistake twice. Generally
it's three times or more.

—MARILYN GREY

When I hear someone sigh that
"Life is hard," I am always tempted
to ask, "Compared to what?"

—SYDNEY HARRIS

Difficulty is the
excuse history never accepts.

—EDWARD R. MURROW

Our greatest glory is not in never failing
but in rising every time we fail.

—EMERSON

It is better to die on your feet
than to live on your knees.

—TALMUD

At a distance, a flock of Great
Northern Geese appears to be guided by
a single lead bird winging courageously
through the oncoming elements. When
the lead bird tires, however, it rotates back
into the formation and another bird flies
at the point position.

LESSON:
Shared burdens are diminished.
Rain or shine, it pays to take turns
doing the hard tasks in life and sharing
both the leadership and the load.

—GREAT NORTHERN GEESE, LESSON V

Life does not accomodate you,
it shatters you. It is meant to and
couldn't do it better. Every seed destroys
its container or else there would be
no growth, no fruition.

—FLORDIA SCOTT MAXWELL

Just don't give up trying
to do what you really want to do.
Where there is love and inspiration,
I don't think you can ever go wrong.

—ELLA FITZGERALD

CELEBRATING THE DIFFERENCE YOU MAKE

BECAUSE OF YOU

WE CAN
DO MORE THAN
APPRECIATE,
WE CAN ENJOY.

If you really want to be happy,
nobody can stop you.

—SISTER MARY TRICKY

Life isn't just the front page—
it's the comics too.

—JIM ALTHOFF

Pure and simple, any person
who is enjoying life is a success.

—WILLIAM FEATHER

CELEBRATING THE DIFFERENCE YOU MAKE

Normal day, let me be
aware of the treasure you are.

—UNKNOWN

Never let the urgent
crowd out the important.

—KELLY CATLIN WALKER

Pause to warm both your hands
before the fire of life.

—WALTER LANDOR

Enjoy yourself.
If you can't enjoy yourself,
enjoy somebody else.

—JACK SCHAEFER

People are more fun than anybody.

—DOROTHY PARKER

Shared joy is double joy.
Shared sorrow is half sorrow.

—SWEDISH PROVERB

CELEBRATING THE DIFFERENCE YOU MAKE

I never lose sight
of the fact that just being is fun.

—KATHARINE HEPBURN

I think of life as a good book.
The further you get into it, the more
it begins to make sense.

—HAROLD KUSHNER

A smile is the light in the window
of your face that tells people that
your heart is at home.

—UNKNOWN

We do not remember days,
we remember moments.

—CESARE PAVESE

Nobody ever has it "all together."
That's like trying to eat
"once and for all."

—MARILYN GREY

Sometimes I would rather have
people take away years of my life
than take away a moment.

—PEARL BAILEY

Where is the yesterday
that worried you so?

—UNKNOWN

There are two sacred days upon
which and about which I never worry.
One of those days is yesterday,
and the other is tomorrow.

—ROBERT BURDETTE

Every evening I turn my
worries over to God. He's going
to be up all night anyway.

—MARY CROWLEY

Life itself is a party. You join after it's
started and you leave before it's finished.

—ELSA MAXWELL

How simple it is to acknowledge
that all the worry in the world could
not control the future. How simple it is to
see that we can only be happy now,
and that there will never be a time
when it is not now.

—GERALD JAMPOLSKY

May you live as long as you want to.
May you want to as long as you live.

—OLD ENGLISH TOAST

CELEBRATING THE DIFFERENCE YOU MAKE

WE CAN DO
MORE THAN LIVE,
WE CAN
BECOME.

Any life is an unfinished story.

—RON PALMER

Retirement at sixty-five is ridiculous.
When I was sixty-five I still had pimples.

—GEORGE BURNS

Whether you are 5 or a 105, you have
a lifetime ahead of you.

—DAN ZADRA

CELEBRATING THE DIFFERENCE YOU MAKE

One is never too old or
too young to yearn.

—C.D. JACKSON

Here is the test to find
whether your mission on earth is
finished. If you're alive it isn't.

—RICHARD BACH

Living is a thing we do,
now or never...which do you?

—PIET HEIN

The best use of life is to spend it
for something that will outlast it.

—WILLIAM JAMES

Each of us will one day be judged by
our standard of life...not by our standard
of living; by our measure of giving...not
by our measure of wealth; by our simple
goodness...not by our seeming greatness.

—WILLIAM ARTHUR WARD

Credentials are not
the same as accomplishments

—ROBERT HALF

CELEBRATING THE DIFFERENCE YOU MAKE

In all my years of counseling
those near death, I've yet to hear
anyone say they wish they had spent more
time at the office.

—RABBI KUSCHNER

A great life is the sum total
of the worthwhile things you've
been doing one by one. Those who
pluck a flower here and there
soon have a bouquet.

—RICHARD BACH

"Be who you are," said the Duchess
to Alice, "or, if you would like it put
more simply, never try to be what you
might have been or could have been other
than what you should have been."

—LEWIS CARROLL

We are not here merely to make
a living. We are here to enrich the world
with a finer spirit of hope and achievement—and we impoverish ourselves
if we forget the errand.

—WOODROW WILSON

Strange, isn't it George,
how each man's life touches
so many others, and when he
isn't around it leaves an awful hole.

—CLARENCE THE ANGEL, "IT'S A WONDERFUL LIFE"

To know even one life has
breathed easier because you have
lived; that is to have succeeded.

—EMERSON

To live in the hearts
we leave behind is not to die.

—THOMAS CAMPBELL

CELEBRATING THE DIFFERENCE YOU MAKE

Time is a very precious gift—
so precious that it is only given
to us moment by moment.

—AMELIA BARR

God must have realized that
humans need to be connected
with the past, so he gave
us memories.

—MIKE RUHLAND

We cannot kill time
without injuring eternity.

—THOREAU

Children, you must remember
something. A person without ambition
is dead. A person with ambition but no
love is dead. A person with ambition and
love for his blessings here on earth is ever
so alive. Having been alive, it won't be
hard in the end to lie down and rest.

—PEARL BAILEY

If I had my life
to live again, I would.

—KOBI YAMADA

THE PLACE
YOU ARE IN
NEEDS YOU
TODAY.

KATHARINE LOGAN

Also available from The Gift of Inspiration Series:

Be Happy.
Remember to Live, Love,
Laugh and Learn

Be the Difference

Brilliance
Uncommon Voices From
Uncommon Women

Commitment to Excellence™
Celebrating the Very Best

Everyone Leads™
It takes each of us to make a
difference for all of us™

Expect Success

Forever Remembered™
A Gift for the Grieving Heart™

I Believe in You™
To your heart, your dream and
the difference you make

Little Miracles™
To renew your dreams,
lift your spirits, and strengthen
your resolve™

Reach for the Stars™
Give up the Good to Go
for the Great

Thank You
In appreciation of you,
and all that you do.

To Your Success
Thoughts to Give Wings to
Your Work and Your Dreams

Together We Can™
Celebrating the power of
a team and a dream™

You've Got a Friend
Thoughts to Celebrate
the Joy of Friendship

Whatever It Takes
A Gift to inspire and celebrate
your commitment to excellence